T0090473

JESUS HAS MY BACK...
AND MY FRONT.

Darlene Hostettler

WESTBOW
PRESS®
A DIVISION OF THOMAS NELSON
& ZONDERVAN

WestBow Press books may be ordered through booksellers or by contacting:

WestBow Press
A Division of Thomas Nelson & Zondervan
1663 Liberty Drive
Bloomington, IN 47403
www.westbowpress.com
844-714-3454

ISBN: 979-8-3850-0953-4 (sc)
ISBN: 979-8-3850-0954-1 (e)

Library of Congress Control Number: 2023919157

Print information available on the last page.

WestBow Press rev. date: 10/12/2023

Dedication

I would like to dedicate this book to my parents and one of my best friends who have all experienced cancer.

My mother died of pancreatic cancer in 2014 and my father had colon cancer in 2013 and survived it, he passed at the age of 91 in 2020.

My dear friend BJ lost her battle with terminal pancreatic cancer, she has been such a great inspiration to all of those around her.

I thank God she is my friend forever.

I miss them every day and praise God I had them in my lives for as long as I did.

Jesus had my back….and my front!

Table of Contents

Introduction

Let me give you a bit of the history of Bill and me.

We are Christians. We believe in Jesus Christ as our personal savior, we met in 1985 and were married September 20, 1986.

Life has treated us well; we trust God will provide for us and he has.

Then we were faced with breast cancer, not just one time, but two and then a third time.

Thank God we have our Lord and our faith to carry us through this journey together.

Chapter 1

Summer 1994, life is short!

*Trust in the Lord with all your
heart and lean not on your own
understanding. Proverbs 3:5*

I had difficulties with my menstrual period since my adolescent years.

We had tried to get pregnant and accepted it was God's plan for us we would not have children. I was diagnosed several years prior with *Polycystic ovary syndrome (PCOS)* is a hormonal disorder common among women of reproductive age. Women with PCOS may have infrequent or prolonged menstrual periods or excess male hormone (androgen) levels. The ovaries may develop numerous small collections of fluid (follicles) and fail to regularly release eggs.

I had seen many doctors over the years and now it was time for the big decision. Surgery, never easy, a hysterectomy.

The Doctor I had been seeing thought it would be good to remove my ovaries.

He also prescribed Hormone Replacement Therapy (HRT) for me.

So, I followed his recommendation and these drugs for about 4 years.

I wish we would have done research before I just blindly started taking these horrible drugs. I am a rule follower, I do what the Dr. says! I regret that we just trusted and did not question these drugs.

And because of it has caused us years of anguish and tears.

Copied from: <u>Hormone therapy: Is it right for you? - Mayo Clinic</u>

HRT: Hormone replacement therapy is medication that contains female hormones. You take the medication to replace the estrogen that your body stops making during menopause. Hormone therapy is most often used to treat common menopausal symptoms, including hot flashes and vaginal discomfort.

Hormone therapy has also been proved to prevent bone loss and reduce fracture in postmenopausal women.

However, there are risks associated with using hormone therapy. These risks depend on the type of hormone therapy, the dose, how long the medication is taken and your individual health risks. For best results, hormone therapy should be tailored to each person and reevaluated every so often to be sure the benefits still outweigh the risks.

What are the basic types of hormone therapy?

Hormone replacement therapy primarily focuses on replacing the estrogen that your body no longer makes after menopause. There are two main types of estrogen therapy:

- **Systemic hormone therapy.** Systemic estrogen — which comes in pill, skin patch, ring, gel, cream, or spray form — typically contains a higher dose of estrogen that is absorbed throughout the body. It can be used to treat any of the common symptoms of menopause.
- **Low-dose vaginal products.** Low-dose vaginal preparations of estrogen — which come in cream, tablet, or ring form — minimize the amount of estrogen absorbed by the body. Because of this, low-dose vaginal preparations are usually only used to treat the vaginal and urinary symptoms of menopause.

If you have not had your uterus removed, your doctor will typically prescribe estrogen along with progesterone or progestin (progesterone-like medication). This is because estrogen alone, when not balanced by progesterone, can stimulate growth of the lining of the uterus, increasing the risk of endometrial cancer. If you have had your uterus removed (hysterectomy), you may not need to take progestin.

What are the risks of hormone therapy?

In the largest clinical trial to date, hormone replacement therapy that consisted of an estrogen-progestin pill (Prempro) increased the risk of certain serious conditions, including:

- Heart disease
- Stroke
- Blood clots
- Breast cancer

Copied from: <u>Hormone therapy: Is it right for you?</u> - Mayo Clinic

Premarin: the intriguing history of a controversial drug

Dwight A Vance Dph [1] Affiliations expand PMID: 23974785

Premarin, a complex of conjugated <u>equine estrogens</u> manufactured by Wyeth for use as hormone replacement therapy in women, was originally developed by the Canadian pharmaceutical firm Ayerst, McKenna, and Harrison. The name Premarin was coined from <u>pregnant mare urine</u>, from which the estrogen complex was isolated. Although the complete composition of Premarin and its active components remains undisclosed or unknown, Wyeth reports that it contains a mixture of ten estrogens. The history of <u>Premarin</u> is entangled in a fascinating story of human intrigue involving ingenuity, influence, controversy, animal rights, competition, money, protection of stockholders, government regulatory power, patient rights, emotions, greed, power, personal and professional freedom, state rights, and even, ultimately, constitutional issues. As the saga of Premarin evolves, it no doubt will continue to be one of the more interesting and compelling stories of the practice of pharmacy. <u>Premarin: the intriguing history of a controversial drug - PubMed (nih.gov)</u>

Chapter 2

Second Opinions Save lives

The Spirit of the LORD will rest on him-the Spirit of wisdom and of understanding, the Spirit of counsel and of power, the Spirit of knowledge and of fear of the Lord. Isaiah 11:2

Throughout my journey I will be giving recommendations for what I used to endure on our journey.

<u>My disclaimer</u>: I used these products or techniques to get through three rounds of cancer, these recommended products or practices in no way prevent or cure cancer. I am giving these ideas for comfort and no medical recommendations.

1. Rely on our Lord Jesus and Prayer.
2. Listen to the Holy Spirit for guidance.
3. Accept support from Family and friends.
4. Follow the doctors' orders.
5. Always follow up with research!

June 1998

We live in Wisconsin; Bill and I had a busy summer planned. You see we had friends coming to visit us from Australia. We had met them on a trip to Hawaii in 1989, our first extended trip since we married in 1986. We were making our life together, happy, healthy, and excited to see what the future held.

I was laying in the tanning bed at the salon where I work. I found a lump inside of my left breast. What is this? I felt my right side, nope not the same. It MUST be a lymph node or something. It was hard like a nut and about the size of an almond.

I waited for Bill to come home from work and told him about it. He said you better call the doctor and get it checked.

So, I scheduled an appointment with a surgeon. I do not remember his name, but I do know he no longer works in local Hospital. He examined me and his exact words, "Oh you women, you wear an underwire bra and get a little lump or bump and think it is something. Go home and take two aspirin."

As I was preparing to leave, I thought, ok, I am good to go! I got an examination by a surgeon, whew, I am glad that is over! I am good!

We had a great visit with our friends and enjoyed our summer!

September 1998; as Christians we know the little voice inside of us is the Holy Spirit giving us guidance. He kept telling me, get a second opinion. Really? I am good, do I really need to do this?

So, I called my Dr. again and asked if I could see another surgeon and this time, I went to St. Elizabeth's in Appleton.

Dr. Stanis examined me and did feel the lump. As I am sitting on the examining table, he is looking right into my eyes. He told me, "I'm 95% sure this is nothing, but do you want me to do a biopsy?"

"Yes! I Do! You are my second opinion!"

The date was set for an open biopsy on Oct. 9,1998. The lump was not visible on a mammogram because of the location of it. So, the procedure was set for Friday, this is a day I will never forget.

Bill drove me to the surgical clinic in Menasha.

It did cross my mind that this could be cancer, but no, it could not be. I am young, I am healthy. I am only 39 years old. Way too young for anything bad to happen.......

A biopsy was performed. I was in the recovery room with Bill, and as I was waking up Dr. Stanis walked in the room.

Well, he said, *"You saved yourself! It is <u>cancer,</u> your scheduled for surgery on Wednesday, after that you will need chemotherapy and radiation."* Boom, just like that!

I am going to die, I thought. This is it; I am going to die; I am going to die. Tears are coming down my face. Bill is crying.

"No No," I said, "I need to go to work and get things in order."

"No, you are not going to work, call them and get ready for surgery on Wednesday." He said and left the room. I was not given a choice in what kind of surgery. No option for a mastectomy currently.

Thankfully, there was an impressive and compassionate nurse in the room with us. She helped me get out of bed and she kept telling me that this is **NOT** a death sentence. *"Cancer is not a death sentence! Many women are surviving breast cancer."*

I am so thankful for this nurse. She was wonderful and helped me.

Meanwhile, Bill got on his phone and started calling everyone to start praying. We had several churches praying for us and my recovery. I felt these prayers and know they were helping us; prayers matter and are effective.

I had told a few close friends and family about my visit. My sister-in-law had a friend who also had this same first surgeon gave her similar news about a lump she had found, but she decided to get a second opinion and found out she also had breast cancer. So did I!

We both wrote letters to the area Hospital about our experiences and the first surgeon who told me to take two aspirins was fired.

I was told later, by my radiation oncologist, if I had waited 6 months longer the cancer would have been in my liver.

My second opinion saved my life!

Chapter 3

Lumpectomy, Chemotherapy and Radiation, UGH!

I will instruct you and teach you in the way you should go; I will counsel you and watch over you. Psalm 32:8

A lumpectomy involves removing the cancer and some of the healthy tissue that surrounds it.

An option for this surgery was not given. I was told it would be a lumpectomy. I was 39 years old, not sure why, a mastectomy was not offered to me.

Surgery: This would be outpatient. Seriously, outpatient? They are taking the lump plus margins around the lump and cutting under my arm pit which included removing 8 Lymph nodes.

You will be fine you can go home. My sister, Patty, and dear friend BJ came along to stay with Bill during my surgery, they were allowed to stay in the pre-operation room until they took me away.

Little did we know, back then my dear friend BJ, would also face cancer in the future.

I was certainly glad they were there! Any support family and friends that are willing to give is always appreciated.

My surgery was about 90 minutes. When I started waking up, I was upright in a chair. I felt a warm presence around me. I felt like two hands were gently on my shoulders. It was my guardian angel or the Holy Spirit letting me know He was there.

A few days after my surgery, we received excellent news!

The cancer was contained to the lump. It was stage one, but it was an aggressive type, so chemotherapy and radiation were the protocol.

The ride home after this surgery was horrible. I could feel every bump in the road, especially driving over all the railroad tracks. If you ever have breast, abdominal, heart or any major surgery, always have a pillow for the ride home. You will hug the pillow to help with the bumps. There is a pillow specifically made for surgery which I did not know about until 2022.

I purchased it online and recommend it for anyone going through breast surgery or any kind of surgery.

The Main reason I bought this pillow was for the pockets for Ice packs, which I found out later I could not use Ice, but I was incredibly happy I had this pillow for my recovery. I also used it in the car for rides to the Doctor. I used my recliner and later in bed to hug when I lay on my side. The cover is also washable.

There are several choices on the market, but I felt this one was the best choice.

Post Mastectomy Pillow - Mastectomy Recovery Breast Reduction | Mastectomy Pillow + Port Pillow + Heart Surgery Pillow | Ice-Pack Ready for Maximum Pain Relief | Washable + Removable Cover- Coral Peach.

Amazon.com: SWISSELITE Mastectomy Pillow, Post Surgery Chest Pillow for Lumpectomy Recovery, Breast Cancer Surgery, Breast Reduction & Augmentation, Port Pacemaker, 3 Cold Therapy Pockets to Support Healing : Health & Household

November 1998

I started Chemotherapy at the Madison Center. This center is affiliated with St. Elizabeth's Hospital.

I did see Dr. Konsik oncologist for chemotherapy. He was a nice man but profoundly professional, serious and matter of fact. I seen him smile once in the twelve chemotherapy sessions I had with him.

I would have 3 months of chemotherapy every other week, six treatments now. Then 6 weeks of radiation therapy, 5 days a week at St. Elizabeth's Hospital. Then 3 more months of chemotherapy. I would complete this course in June of 1999.

I really wish I had learned these tips early on. This is one of the main reasons I am authoring this book.

Chemotherapy Helpful Tips:

- Do not use metal when cooking, no metal tools to stir. When enduring chemotherapy it is likely you will taste metal, this really helps to enjoy food.
- Make food in the microwave with glass.
- Eat with a plastic fork or spoon, your food will taste better.
- Do not drink or eat anything from a can.
- Eat popsicles for headaches, the green flavor was best for me. I have not eaten one since.
- Gel Ice packs or gel caps are great for headaches too.
- Eat what you crave. I craved mashed potatoes, so we bought instant, so it was easier for Bill to prepare.
- Eat small portions more often.
- Pretzels or nuts helped with the nausea.
- Have soft foods on hand and protein drinks for when you are just not hungry.
- Keep fruit juice and Gatorade on hand.
- Eat healthily and walk in the fresh air when you feel up to it.

Radiation therapy was not as difficult to endure. It made me extremely tired. I was blessed not to have my skin burned. I was happy I did not experience nausea with radiation.

The nurses and staff at all these facilities were fabulous!

It took me a while to get through and recover from all the therapies in 1998-1999. But I always had faith we could endure and would live to see much better days.

I did continue to work part time while going through all of this. Sometimes I wonder how I made it through these long months, but I know the Lord was giving me strength and endurance to keep going.

All the prayers and support from our family, friends and our church family are priceless!

What Cancer CANNOT DO!

It cannot cripple LOVE.
It cannot shatter HOPE.
It cannot corrode FAITH.
It cannot destroy PEACE.
It cannot kill FREINDSHIP.
It cannot suppress MEMORIES.
It cannot silence COURAGE.
It cannot invade the SOUL.
It cannot steal ETERNAL LIFE!
It cannot conquer the SPIRIT.
It cannot lesson the POWER OF THE RESURRECTION.
-Unknown Author

Copied From: www.creanoso.com

You do not know how strong you are until strong is all you have.
-Bob Marley

With Jesus, we are stronger than the storm.
There is always something to be thankful for.
Always try to find the silver lining.
-Darlene Hostettler

Chapter 4

Angels are among us!!

*And there appeared an angel unto him
from heaven, strengthening him. Luke 22:43*

I was diagnosed with breast cancer on Oct. 9, 1998. Soon after surgery, I started with chemotherapy followed by radiation therapy; it was a long nine-month battle.

It was a Friday morning in November, the day after my second chemotherapy treatment, I was feeling very nauseous and hugging my brown *Russ Teddy bear*, my girlfriend, BJ, had given me when I became sick. I was lying on the couch in my pajamas, praying to God to please send *His Angels* down to take the nausea away.

Moments later the doorbell rang; I went to the door to find a friend, Rita, who had come to visit. She said, *"Oh you're not feeling well, I'll come back another time."* *"Please come in,"* I said, *"a visit from a friend will help more than you know."* She came in and we began to visit *Angel #1*.

Minutes later, the bell rang again, how nice I thought, another "visitor." To my surprise the floral delivery person from Schumacher's Flowers Store was standing at my door, but this time he was not bringing flowers, he was holding a wrapped gift. How thoughtful, someone sent me a gift! He handed it to me and was on his way. I proceeded back to my friend, excited about the gift. I opened it. It was a *beautiful white Angel holding a brown teddy bear, with blonde hair!*

It was sent from a client and friend, Mary Beth, who had just found out I was battling cancer. I was so touched by this act of kindness, knowing God had spoken to her heart to buy this for me. I know this was not a coincidence; *this is a message from God.*

I called her on the phone, "*Mary Beth, thank you so much for the Angel!*" I continued to tell her about my prayer and how I was holding a teddy bear and the angel she had sent was also holding a teddy bear. She said "*OH MY! I have goose bumps!*" I asked her what made her decide to send the Angel?

Mary Beth said, "*She walked around the flower shop three times, unsure what to send, and it seemed the Angel was calling her name.*"

We were both very moved and touched by this event, knowing God had spoken to her heart and He *does hear and answer our prayers.*

My prayer was answered, the nausea went away.

With strong faith and the support of my family and friends, I am a cancer survivor. **Angels are among us!**

The angel of the LORD encamps around those who fear him, and he delivers them. For the angel of the LORD is a guard; he surrounds and defends all who fear him. Psalm 34:7

Chapter 5

Getting back to normal

Give thanks to the LORD, for he is good.
His love endures forever. Psalms 136:1

It is hard to believe that life has a way of going by too fast.

I went back to full time work. Stepped away from managing the salon. Bill and I had purchased a small cabin in the north woods of Wisconsin and planned to update it and make it a year-round destination for fun, rest, and relaxation.

We have met many fabulous friends and enjoy our time as much as possible at "Da Cabin."

Enjoy your life every day!

Travel when you are healthy and have a chance, go, and experience what is available.

Your life could change in an instant!

Darlene Hostettler

Bill and I are very blessed to have been able to travel also.

We grew in our faith and God has blessed us.

We had 22 years enjoying life, then we went back in time to 1998.

Chapter 6

NOT AGAIN! May 2020

But when He, the Spirit of truth, comes, He will guide you into all the truth; for he will not speak on His own initiative, but whatever He hears, He will speak; and he will disclose to you what is to come. John 16:13

I was very diligent about getting my yearly physicals and mammograms. After my chemotherapy was finished, I was on a three then six then nine-month schedule for my tests. Then after a one year, the mammograms were performed yearly.

In May of 2020, during the worldwide Covid-19 pandemic, I had my scheduled mammogram. A few days later I received a call that I would need a core biopsy.

OH Great! If you have ever experienced this procedure, you will know it is very unpleasant. They place your breast into the mammogram machine, freeze it and proceed to inject a pencil size probe with a blade on the end of it, to remove the tissue they need to examine.

Well, I told the Doctor to give me the double dose to freeze my breast, he did not. *"You'll be fine"* he said. Well, the tissue they needed was very deep in my breast, about an inch from my ribs. So, I told him I could feel burning. He said, *"You'll be fine, we're almost done."* Tears ran down my face. REALLY? I thought can I put one of your body parts in a vice, freeze it, probe it with a blade, and tell you, we are almost finished?

Sorry, sometimes you just need to hear the brutal details.

Days later, I received a call from the clinic, where I had been going for many years. Except *for this* experience, I have been incredibly happy with them. I had to change where I was getting medical treatment because of an insurance change.

So, I received the call from them and was told it was cancer. *"Are you alone"*? he asked. *"Yes, I am."*

"I'm very sorry to inform you, it is cancer, and they will be scheduling you with a surgeon, for a consultation."

I was numb. After 22 years why would this be happening again? Was the stress from the pandemic too much?

Dealing with life can be stressful.

Within minutes, I received a call from Laura, my new navigator. This clinic offers a navigator to help you get through the cancer process. Laura made appointments for me and assisted me with several things during this journey.

Because of the pandemic, I did not get to meet her, until much later in my journey. She is a wonderful gal, and really listened to me. She kept asking me if I was all right. Bill will be home soon.

She asked if I wanted a female or male surgeon. I requested a female, so she set up an appointment.

I am not going to mention this Dr.'s name, because I did not care for her, and I will tell you why.

A disclaimer: if you are not happy with your medical Dr. or the facility, you have a right to go elsewhere. I am a firm believer in everything that happens for a reason and The Holy Spirit gives you a warm fuzzy feeling or a bad feeling in your spirit if you need to make a change with any decision you need to make.

So, I went to see this first female Dr. for a consultation; my sister was there with me.

First off, she was late for my appointment.

After she examined me, she made several negative comments.

She was annoyed that I was asking her so many questions.

I asked, *"What would you do if this was you?"*

Her response was," *I don't care about a breast."*

I asked, *"What would you recommend if this was your sister?"*

"Why are you asking questions?" was her retort. Really, I thought, isn't this a consultation? I did not care for her bedside manner.

I did have the genetic testing done in her office and found out days later that I did not have the Barca Gene.

That would have determined my decision to get a bilateral mastectomy, but that was not the case.

So, after that visit, I called my navigator Laura, and she scheduled me for another consultation with Dr. Cynthia Geocaris.

When you have breast cancer for the second time, there are enormous decisions you are faced with; Lumpectomy, single mastectomy, or double mastectomy.

This was our reasoning for another Lumpectomy.

It had been 22 years since my first diagnosis. If I can go another 22 years, I will be in my eighties, then at that time I can decide if major surgery is needed.

I met with Dr. Geocaris and was happy with her demeanor and personality. Her office staff was also genuinely nice. So, my surgery was planned for June 24, 2020, at Theda Care Hospital, Neenah, WI. We decided on a lumpectomy.

The surgery went well, and I was sent home the same day. They took a margin, extra tissue around the cancer, to send out to be evaluated. The margin came back clear! Praise God!

I did not need chemotherapy or radiation therapy because they found the cancer early. I will need to get my mammograms every 3 months, following my doctors' orders.

There was a time where they thought radiation would be a promising idea, but when I met with a radiation oncologist, she made the decision it was not needed. Another great blessing!

2020 was a difficult year. My father's health was declining because of the pandemic, we were not allowed to visit him in the assisted living facility where he had been living for a few years. We could call, visit him through his window, but most of us would Facetime him.

Thank God, he was very savvy and smart, he knew how to use a smart phone.

My Dad passed away on August 20, 2020. I miss him every day.

Christmas 2018 and Oct. 2019 we had dinner at my niece's culinary school. Dad, my sister Patty, and niece Haley.

Chapter 7

Wait and See

These are my favorite verses.

Praise the Lord, O my soul; all my inmost being, praise His holy name. Praise the Lord, O my soul, and forget not all His benefits – who forgives all your sins and heals all your diseases, who redeems your life from the pit and crowns you with love and compassion, who satisfies your desires with good things so that your youth is renewed like the eagle's. Psalm 103: 1-5

October 2021 I was scheduled for my routine mammogram. After having two lumpectomies, I had a lot of scar tissue.

After the mammogram, the radiologist doctor, who read the mammogram wanted to speak with me. This is usually not good. He came into the room and told me there were suspicious cells. Would you like to have a biopsy done now or what until your next mammogram?

I decided to wait until January. The holidays are coming soon, and I knew that if surgery were required in the future, I would not have it done until January.

So, we scheduled my next mammogram for January 2022.

Chapter 8
Third Times a Charm?

*I will instruct you and teach you in the
way you should go; I will counsel you
and watch over you. Psalm 32:8*

I had my mammogram and another needle biopsy in January 2022.

On January 31st, I received a call from Theda Care and was informed they wanted to see me.

My response was, *"Ok, this is not my first rodeo. Please just tell me is it good or bad"?* She said she could not tell me. *"Well, you just did."* I replied.

I requested that my doctor put a note in "mythedacare," a portal for Theda Care patients to make appointments, contact your doctor, pay your bill, and ask for prescription refills. It is really a convenient and useful tool especially during a pandemic!

So, she sent a message, the needle biopsy results show cancer, she would recommend a mastectomy and reconstruction at this time and would like to see me. Please let us know when you are available to come to discuss your options.

And there you have it, here we go again! Not too many choices this time. God will guide and give me strength to endure this journey.

Chapter 9

Jesus is the warrior carrying us through this battlefield called cancer!

And we know that in all things God works for the good of those who love him, who have been called according to his purpose. Romans 8:28

My surgery, a bilateral mastectomy, was planned for March 4, 2022. The day before surgery I had to see plastic surgeon Dr. VanYe. He had to mark my breasts for surgery, so Dr. Geocaris could follow his plan. While he was marking me, he found an infected cyst. So, he canceled the surgery. This made me incredibly sad; I was physically and emotionally ready for the surgery, but God was protecting me in more ways than I could imagine at this time.

I had all seven of my prescriptions ready waiting for my recovery. One of them was an antibiotic Keflex, Cephalexin.

The nurse from Dr. VanYe's office called and told me to take the Keflex for the full 10 days and they would get back to me on rescheduling my surgery. Great, no problem. I had mixed emotions about the surgery being postponed. Little did I know *Jesus had my back and my front,* like always. He had my back in many ways.

So, I took the full 10-day course of the antibiotic. I had returned to work for the month of March. I woke up during the night on an early Tuesday morning with what felt like a fever, so I took a couple of Tylenol and went back to bed. I normally get up between 6:00 – 6:30 AM, it was nearly 8:00 AM when Bill came to wake me. "*Are you ok?*" Yes, I answered, just feeling a little feverish. I will get up now. I went to the bathroom to get ready for the day, On Tuesday's I normally began work about 12:30, so I did not need to get up early.

I looked in the mirror and screamed! I had a full-blown rash all over my body! It looked like I had measles! "*Bill, come in here! OH, GOOD GRIEF! WHAT'S GOING ON!*" He told me to get in the shower. That did not help. I had an allergic reaction to the Keflex, antibiotic.

I called Dr. VanYe's office, and they recommended I call my primary Dr. Adam Olson. So, I called and got an appointment with his associate, Scott Schuldes NP. I went in with my rash and all, he was genuinely nice and prescribed a steroid for the pain, at this point the rash looked terrible, but did not start to itch until after I had seen him. This side effect of itching was one of the worst medical experiences I have ever had, IT WAS HORRIBLE. Right up there with Chemotherapy and Covid, that I had in Jan. 2021.

Darlene Hostettler

I proceeded to get advice from family and friends to take oatmeal baths. These did give me some relief. At 2:30 AM I was soaking in the bathtub praying to God to take this awful itching from me. On Friday, I called my Dr. again asking him for a recommendation to help with this itching. They prescribed a cream that finally gave me relief. Thank you, Jesus, for saving me from this horrible itching.

Bill came to this realization, #1 thank God you had this reaction before your surgery you would not have been able to take your oatmeal baths if you had had your surgery, no bathing with incisions.

#2, He saved me from the infection, which if the cyst had not surfaced, could have gone into my blood, and caused major infection or sepsis, which can be fatal.

After Avena oatmeal baths, three prescriptions and Benadryl, the rash disappeared. It took six full days, and I am very thankful my skin did not blister. I know God protected me. If I had had this reaction after my surgery, I am not sure I would have had the strength to endure it!

I had a taste of "hades" and never want another! No oatmeal baths there!!

Jesus had my back and my front! Amen.

Chapter 10

The Surgery

Do not be anxious about anything, but in everything, by prayer and petition, with thanksgiving, present your requests to God. Philippians 4:6

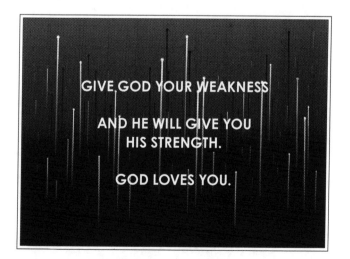

GIVE GOD YOUR WEAKNESS

AND HE WILL GIVE YOU HIS STRENGTH.

GOD LOVES YOU.

After I was healed from the horrible allergic reaction, the surgery was rescheduled for Friday, April 1, 2022. April Fools, this was no joke.

Since March 2020, the world has been going through a "Pandemic". So, with every Dr. appointment, Bill was not allowed to come in the clinic, I had to answer questions like; if I had been exposed, did I have a fever....and of course wear a mask throughout the entire visit. So, it was April 2022, the covid restrictions were starting to relax a bit, so Bill was allowed to be with me in the hospital!

Thank you, Jesus!

The night before surgery I was very anxious. I was praying to God. The Lord placed on my heart this vision of Christ praying the night before he was crucified. Please Father take this from me. My same prayer. Jesus could go through the crucifixion; I could make through this surgery with his guidance and love. And I did.

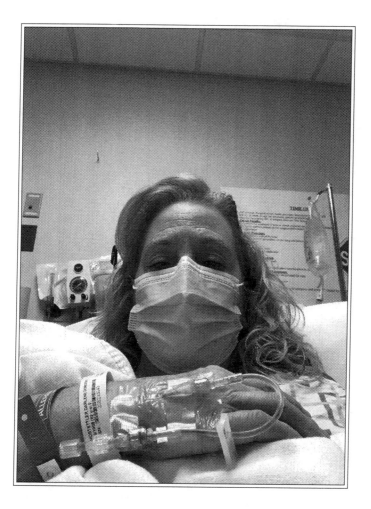

We needed to arrive by 9:30 AM at Theda Care Neenah Hospital.

They prepared me and took me in by 11:00 AM, it was a four to five-hour surgery. The Dr.'s told Bill the surgery could not have gone better.

I returned to the in-patient hospital room at 5:00 PM. I was connected to Oxygen, blood pressure monitor, wound vacuum pump, leg pumps and IV. Bill was a bit overwhelmed. We prayed together and I told him, I have two excellent friends who are Registered Nurses, who told me they would come and help us if we needed anything. Plus, Bill's sister, Linda, is a C.N.A, who also offered to help, and they all did come when we called on them.

Bill stayed until about 8:00 PM that night and a little later my cousin, Linda and her husband walked in for a visit. I was surprisingly awake, and it was genuinely nice they came to visit. They gave me a sticker that read, "God Loves You," so I placed it on my water bottle. Then it got interesting.

*I will instruct you and teach you in the
way you should go; I will counsel you
and watch over you. Psalm 32:8*

I was surprisingly awake, and the staff was trying to manage my pain, with Tylenol and Oxycodone. Little did I know Oxycodone is a stimulant for me, keeping me wide awake! I truly got little sleep if any, that whole night. The RN, Allison, walked into my room to check on me. She saw the "God Loves You" sticker on my water bottle.

She asked, "So God Loves You, how do you know that's true?"

I replied," *God loves everyone, he loves you!*" "*How do you know this?*" "I received the words from the Holy Spirit, "because *the Bible tells us He loves us. He wants us to believe in Him.*"

The conversation went on and she wanted to know more. We talked for 45 minutes. I told her "*God works the night shift*," she giggled.

She accepted Christ as her Savior by saying this prayer.

I am a sinner. I accept and believe in Jesus Christ as my Savior; I repent of my sins.

She said she had some unresolved sins. I told her "God forgives all *sins.*"

We discussed private things about family, and she wanted to know of a church she could attend with her family.

Over the next few days, I found her a church in the city she lives in. I told her I would not be a stalker, a fanatical lady or bother her about any of this. She seemed happy and content.

Reason #3; God postponed my surgery so I could witness to this young lady and bring her to our Lord.

In the morning when she came in to say good-bye to me and introduced me to the morning RN, Tracy. It was comical, "Be careful, you are going to get Jesus in here!"

She said, "I already have Jesus, I'm a Lutheran!"

"That's wonderful!" I said with a smile.

Darlene Hostettler

Photo before leaving Theda Care Hospital.

Chapter 11

Recovery

---

*And my God will meet all your needs
according to his glorious riches in
Christ Jesus. Philippians 4:19*

I had started a *CaringBridge* sight to keep family and friends up to date on our journey. It was a wonderful way to keep folks informed who wanted to know how things were going. They log in as a visitor or a follower and will get notification when there is a new journal entry. I recommend this site; it is user friendly.

This was my *CaringBridge* journal entry for April 2, 2022.

We got home Saturday at about 2:00 PM. So glad to get a good sleep last night.

So thankful for Bill and his compassion. He is a wonderful man and managing this nurse role very well.

I am so grateful to my family and friends for all the prayers and acts of kindness. We are managing all the medications and daily shots. Please continue to pray for healing and pain free recovery.

> *Give thanks in all circumstances,*
> *for this is God's will for you in Christ*
> *Jesus. 1 Thessalonians 5:18*

My recovery was challenging but rewarding.

I had the wound vacuum for the first 10 days and the drain tubes in for 18 days after surgery. More about these great inventions later.

I had so many prayers, get well cards, visits, gifts, meals and support from friends and family. It was so touching and heartwarming. God has blessed us with so many wonderful people in our lives, *I am so blessed to have each one of them.*

I could not lay flat, so I had to sleep in my recliner for the first 5 weeks, it was the most comfortable and I did sleep after I realized the Oxycodone, keep me wired, so I stop taking it at night. Managing the seven medications was a challenge until my friend Dawn RN came and helped us get them on schedule.

I do not think the medical personnel realize the challenges an average person faces when we are sent home from surgery with the instruction list and managing all these medications.

Thank God for Dawn RN, Linda RN and sister Linda who came and helped. It is good to have nurses in your tribe.

Chapter 12

Excellent News

I will praise you, O LORD, with all my heart;
I will tell of all your wonders. Psalms 9:1

April 6, 2022, CaringBridge Entry

Excellent news! I just received the call from Surgical Associates; the pathology results for my tissue margins are all NEGATIVE!! I am so happy I am crying! ♡

God bless and thank you for all your prayers and blessings!

This is my third time that I endured surgery for cancer. The stress and anxiety related to these experiences can be overwhelming. I am so thankful I have the Lord to give me the strength that I have needed throughout my life. I am grateful for my salvation.

NOTHING FEELS BETTER

THAN KNOWING
GOD LOVES YOU,

THAT HE IS ALWAYS
THERE FOR YOU

AND THAT HE WILL ALWAYS

TAKE CARE OF YOU.

Chapter 13

Recovery appointments!

*For I know the plans I have for you,"
declares the LORD, "plans to prosper
you and not to harm you, plans to give
you hope and a future. Jeremiah 29:12*

I had a Dr. Appointment today and all is well. The cancer was found early. Praise the Lord!! I will not need chemotherapy or radiation!!

The wound vacuum and drain tubes are still in place but these are to help my incisions heal.

I will see both surgeons again next week Tuesday.

Bill took me to get my hair shampooed and braided at a dear friends' Jacque's salon. What a TREAT!!

I am so grateful for all your prayers, visits, food, flowers, cards, calls, and blessings. No words can express how thankful and blessed I feel!

Darlene Hostettler

JESUS HAS MY BACK...AND MY FRONT.

49

THANK YOU!

Just sharing memories that have given me encouragement to "fight like a girl!"

If you do not have the devotion book <u>Jesus Calling by Sarah Young</u>, I highly recommend it.

The photo of me I am sharing to show you my "wound vacuum" that is attached to my chest to help my incision heal.

The funny thing is it makes farting noises! Any of you that know our Heidi runs out of the room when she hears someone pass gas, it is hysterical! She knows what comes after the sound! LOL

So, since my surgery I have had to muffle this "wound vac" device under my blanket or Heidi is hesitant to come near me!

Our dear family and friends have been so supportive you all have made my heart happy! ♡

Thank you!

*Give thanks in all circumstances,
for this is God's will for you in Christ
Jesus. 1 Thessalonians 5:18*

A dear friend, Mary, bought Bill a pink smock yesterday!

He was a good sport to wear for this photo.

So cute!

We also had a wonderful meal brought on Monday from a dear friend, Mary! We appreciate all meals, visits, cards, texts, calls and mostly prayers!

A funny story, an incredibly good friend advised me to buy depends for the ride home after surgery. I hesitated but decided to listen to her advice. You may not have control after surgery, and it will save you grief. So, I wore one home.

After we were home, Bill helped me with my shower. My clothes were on a pile on the bathroom floor, I asked him to throw them in the washer with the towels. Little did I know the "depends" were in the pile.

That afternoon my friend, Dawn, came over to help with my medication schedule with which we were struggling. Before she left, I asked her if she could transfer the clothes to the dryer. She opened the washer and said, "It looks like it snowed in here!" "Oh, My Goodness! What is that?" Little did I know, the "depends" had exploded in the washer and left tiny white particles all over everything. We both had a good laugh and thankfully the particles rolled right off the rest of the clothes. No harm to the rest of the clothing.

Chapter 14

It is only tape!

For I know the plans I have for you,"
declares the LORD, "plans to prosper
you and not to harm you, plans to give
you hope and a future. Jeremiah 29:12

Today was a busy day. I had appointments with both surgeons.

It was a surprise when the general surgeon said my wound vacuum would be removed today! I did not realize my skin was still sensitive from the allergic reaction I had in March.

Now if you are not familiar with a wound vacuum, the best description I can give; think about two thin pieces of foam, duck taped to your "chest" over your 11th day incisions.

Imagine a huge super tight band aid. They said, *"Ripping it off fast is less painful." "Hey, no problem it's only tape!!"* I cried during the removal. Temporary pain. It was over quickly.

On a positive note, my incisions look great! I am healing, praise the Lord!! The Lord has blessed me with excellent Surgeons and medical staff!

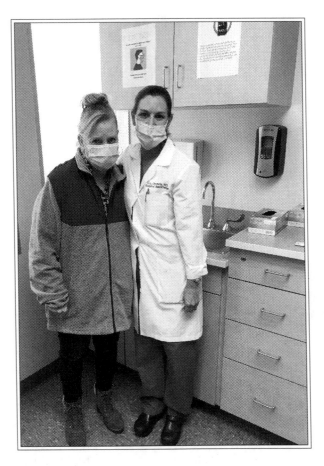

My general surgeon.

I cried like a baby when I got into the car. Bill asked me if I wanted to go for ice cream. He did not need to ask me twice.

Chapter 15

Happy Easter!!

From my Caring Bridge: April 16, 2022

Happy Easter Everyone,

It has been a few days since I posted so I thought it would be good to give an update.

I am so thankful I am gaining strength every day. I do attribute this to my fabulous caregiver Bill, all the prayers said for us, the wonderful blessings of food, the lovely gifts, flowers, and the welcomed visits.

I praise God for all of you! I attached a photo of our niece *Sheila with Heidi* who came equipped with coffee, muffins, and a lovely gift for our visit today.

For my Father's will is that everyone who looks to the Son and believes in him shall have eternal life, and I will raise him up on the last day.

John 6:40

Darlene Hostettler

Because we know that the one who raised the Lord Jesus from the dead will also raise us with Jesus and present us with you in his presence.

2 Corinthians 4:14

Happy Easter! †

Chapter 16

Removing Tubes

Give thanks to the LORD, for he is good.
His love endures forever. Psalms 136:1

Tuesday was an enjoyable day!

I had an appointment with Dr. VanYe to have my drain tubes removed. I was very apprehensive and preparing for pain. I do not handle pain well.

But I was pleasantly surprised, the nurse said take a deep breath and she removed them one at a time, and I had NO PAIN!! I certainly appreciate I had no idea there were at least twelve -18" tubes inside of me! No wonder I had "zingers" going on!

Again, it is all temporary and so THANKFUL for my healing and blessings!

With each day I am building strength!

So thankful for all the prayers and blessings!

Dr. VanYe, my excellent plastic surgeon.

And we know that all things work
together for good to them that love
God, to them who are the called
according to his purpose. Romans 8:28

Chapter 17

SO THANKFUL!

Give thanks to the LORD, for he is good.
His love endures forever. Psalms 136:1

I had a Dr. appointment yesterday and my healing is on schedule. I am so grateful for gaining daily strength and my healing recovery. I am 5 weeks out from surgery today.

I am so grateful for prayers, visits, cards, texts, meals, and gifts since my surgery.

A friend dropped by for a visit Wed. and brought me "Clancy bear." You can see him in the photo with all my get-well cards I received during our journey. Heidi was so excited about Clancy, she thought he was her new toy, too funny! I am so appreciative for all your prayers and thoughtfulness! Sending healing prayers out for folks battling cancer.

Chapter 18

One day, one step, one breath at a time

I went in weekly for my expander fills to stretch my skin so I could have my reconstruction surgery, April – July, which means I will have the expanders removed and implants surgically placed.

I chose this type of surgery because the recovery time was shorter. I trusted Dr. VanYe, at our consultation he told me in 25 years he never had to remove any implants.

Chapter 19
Reconstruction

And my God will meet all your needs according to his glorious riches in Christ Jesus. Philippians 4:19

My reconstruction surgery was scheduled for December 20, 2022.

I came down with a fever from Sunday into Monday. My temperature was 100.5 before we left for surgery that morning. We prayed on the way to The Center; it was a very wintry morning. When we were escorted in by nurse Katie, she took my temperature, and it was ninety-seven.' PRAISE THE LORD!! The surgery was on! Everything went well and we were heading home by early afternoon. I could not believe it!

I had four weeks off from work for recovery and I was glad I did.

I am healing well and every day the pain is less.

Darlene Hostettler

I cannot believe it has been a week since my surgery. We had a wonderful Christmas celebration at my sister's home, it is great to spend Christmas with family.

I have been gaining strength with each day.

Today I had my one-week checkup, and I am healing well. I did receive unwelcome news today; Dr. VanYe removed a spot on my chest area, while in surgery and he sent the biopsy in, and the results were Basal cell carcinoma skin cancer. We discussed this prior, and he was suspicious that it could be Basal cell, which is a less invasive form of skin cancer. Melanoma is an invasive type of skin cancer. Anytime I hear cancer it does set me back, but I know Jesus has my back! It brings me closer to Him.

Thank you to everyone for all your prayers, support, cards, visits, and kindness. Bill and I appreciate each of you!

God's richest blessings for a healthy, happy, and prosperous New Year.

YOU DON'T HAVE TO
FIGURE IT
ALL OUT THIS MINUTE,
TAKE ONE BREATH,
ONE HOUR,
ONE STEP,
ONE DAY AT A TIME.
GOD IS WITH YOU.

Chapter 20

Lessons Learned

God is our refuge and strength, an ever-present help in trouble. Psalm 46:1

If I have learned anything from cancer.

Life can change in an instant.

As I am working on my book today, my dear friend, BJ, who was diagnosed with terminal cancer in January 2023.

They were on their way this morning for her to have a procedure done for pain management, when her husband started having chest pain, so they drove to the ER. He did have a heart attack and she was examined also for pain she experienced. They checked her for a blood clot. Praise our Lord the ER was nearby, and they could save his life! BJ did not have a blood clot and she had her pain management procedure done the next morning.

Dear Lord, give them peace and courage, I pray in your precious name of Jesus. Amen!

Do not be anxious about anything, but in everything, by prayer and petition, with thanksgiving, present your requests to God.
Philippians 4:6

Her words.

"I have this to say...life guarantees ups and downs, trails and tribulation....but if you are in a constant state of "nothing ever goes right"...here's my advice...try God... really...the Bible has everything we need to know on how to be a good mate, parent, child, employee, friend, ...etc...so there it is...the big JC...is your answer."

BJ Jaeckels

My dear friend BJ, went to meet Jesus on May 27, 2023

Enjoy heaven my dear friend, I miss you! Until we meet again!

Bill, Darlene, Andrew, Terry, and Troy.

Awesome friends of ours, who have been a great encouragement for Bill and me.

O taste and see that the LORD is good: blessed is the man that trusteth in him. Psalm 34:8

Oct. 2022, living again and enjoying life.

I will praise you, O LORD, with all my heart;
I will tell of all your wonders. Psalms 9:1

DON'T BE AFRAID TO GET BACK UP AGAIN,
TO LIVE AGAIN, TO LOVE AGAIN, AND TO
DREAM AGAIN. DON'T LET A HARD LESSON
HARDEN YOUR HEART. LET YOUR RIPPLE
SHINE. Darlene Hostettler

pngtree.com

Walk by faith, not by sight. 2 Corinthians 5:7

Darlene Hostettler

You shall walk in all the ways which the LORD your God has commanded you, that you may live and that it may be well with you, and that you may prolong your days in the land which you shall possess. Deut. 5:33

For my Father's will is that everyone who looks to the Son and believes in him shall have eternal life, and I will raise him up on the last day. John 6:40

Thank you for reading my book and God Bless every one of you. Please pass it along to encourage anyone facing cancer.

I trust the next chapters of my life because I know the author!

God's Richest Blessings,
Darlene Hostettler

Printed in the United States
by Baker & Taylor Publisher Services